The Coming Great Awakening

Dr. Michael H Yeager

Dr. Michael H Yeager

iv

DEDICATION

To those who are hungry and desperate for a mighty move of God. To the bride of Christ who is making herself ready. To the Holy church, the sheep of JESUS.

Revelation 22:16-18
King James Version (KJV)

16 I Jesus have sent mine angel to testify unto you these things in the churches. I am the root and the offspring of David, and the bright and morning star.

17 And the Spirit and the bride say, Come. And let him that heareth say, Come. And let him that is athirst come. And whosoever will, let him take the water of life freely.

CONTENTS

ACKNOWLEDGMENTS

All Praise onto God the Father, God the son, God the Holy Ghost, the three in one.

Ephesians 3:19-21
King James Version (KJV)

19 And to know the love of Christ, which passeth knowledge, that ye might be filled with all the fulness of God.

20 Now unto him that is able to do exceeding abundantly above all that we ask or think, according to the power that worketh in us,

21 Unto him be glory in the church by Christ Jesus throughout all ages, world without end. Amen.

Dr. Michael H Yeager

CHAPTER 1
SIGNIFICANT VISITATION

I would like to share with you an amazing visitation that I had on February the 20, 2012. On the 18 of February, I celebrated my 56th birthday. The 37th year of being born again.(I v been a pastor since 1977) I set my heart to seek God, trusting to totally separate my mind, my heart, completely free from all knowledge but God's Word, and only that information which I need in order to fulfill the will of God. From the minute I set my mind and heart to be completely given over to the Lord, great anticipation and expectation began to rise in me. On the third day I went to bed meditating upon God's WORD. The dream I am about to share with you was more than a dream. All of my five senses and physical being experienced that which I am about to share.

In this Dream I found myself standing outside of a small town on top of a grass covered hill. Other saints (some that I am familiar with) were gathered together there with me. (There were seven to a dozen of us). The stars were shining brightly from above. There was no moon this particular night. It was a beautiful warm summer evening. You could hear the night life all around us. The crickets and frogs were joined together in their song. As I was standing there with the gathering of these saints, I sensed in my heart that something astounding was about to happen in the heavens above us.

Dr. Michael H Yeager

I perceived that the heavens were about to be shaken. I perceived in my heart that it was necessary for all of us to immediately get on our backs, and look into the heavens. When I shared this with those who were gathered together with me on the Hill, they all agreed and we immediately laid down on our backs. Within just a matter of minutes the heavens above us exploded into activity. It was as if a great battle was unfolding in the heavens. There was destruction happening throughout the sky as if it was in great travail and pain, and yet that there was a birthing, a coming forth of life and a new heaven.

What we watched unfold before us was mind boggling and dumbfounding. Frightening and yet exhilarating. It seemed to go on for hours. And as fast as it had begun, it was over with. All of us present slowly arose to our feet. We were so overwhelmed and dumbfounded with what we saw that none of us could talk. We were utterly speechless. Our hearts were filled with wonder and amazement. I perceived that all who were present knew that God was revealing himself to the human race in a way He had not previously demonstrated. That God was doing something in the heavens and the earth that humanity had not yet seen or experienced.

We all dispersed from the hilltop slowly going our own separate ways. I found myself on a sidewalk beginning to enter into a small community. The streets were filled with people looking into the heavens. I could see great fear filling the faces on those who were speaking back and forth to one another in whispers about

what all of this could mean? I continued to walk down
the sidewalk not speaking to anyone. The atmosphere
was filled with a sense of great fear and anticipation.

As I entered deeper into this town, once again I
sense that something was about to happen. (Now this is
where it really begins to get interesting.)The minute I
perceived something dramatic was about to happen I
stopped. There were tall buildings off to my right and left
hand, which you would typically find in a small town.

I looked up into the heavens, and it seemed as if to
me the heavens were made from a parchment. I watched
in amazement as if an invisible hand was rolling up the
heavens like they were a newspaper, or a parchment. And
then as if the heavens were insignificant, it was set aside
as if it were nothing.

The minute this took place behind where the heavens
had been there was now an innumerable multitude of the
heavenly host. The Saints of all ages dressed in glistening
white, were gathered with the angelic armies behind
them. In the midst was the Heavenly Father sitting upon a
great white throne. God the Father was so huge in size
that all else looked small in comparison. All of those who
were present including the Father seemed to be looking
off to my right.

As I looked in the direction in which they were
gazing to my amazement there was the Lamb of God. His
wool was glistening white as snow. He was lying upon
His side as if He had been slain. His backside was away

from me, His underside toward me. And out from His rib, it seemed to be His third rib, from his side flowed a stream of bright shimmering living, quickening blood. Directly in front of His body there had formed a pool of this living blood. I knew there was no bottom to this pool of blood. It is hard to explain what I sensed in my heart as I looked upon His, the Lamb of God's precious living blood.

As I was looking upon this pool of precious blood, I felt something manifest itself in my right hand. I looked down, and there in my right hand was a branch, a ROD. (This was the specific word that came to my mind)This was not just any ordinary Rod. It was absolutely straight, and it was made of Olive Wood, seemingly seven feet tall. (These are things I just knew to be true)

Immediately I knew what I was to do with this Rod in my right hand. I lifted this Rod towards the pool of blood in the heavens. To my amazement it seemed to be just the right length to reach into the blood. This blood was in the heavens, and yet this seven foot Rod was able to reach the precious blood of Jesus.

I put the end of the Rod right into this pool of living blood. The blood immediately flowed to the end of the Rod. This living blood wrapped itself around the end of the Rod as if it was in absolute oneness with the Rod. Then with my right hand I pulled the Rod back towards me. Once the Rod was back into my Realm (I do not know how else to explain it). I directed the end of the Rod towards my mouth. It looked as if the blood was

4

going to fall off from the end of the Rod. But not a drop fell to the ground.

I opened my mouth wide, and stuck the end of the Rod with the Living Blood into my mouth. I drank all of the blood which had been on the Rod. The very moment that I drank the blood, it was as if Power exploded inside of me, knocking me flat on my back like a dead man. It slammed me violently to the ground. I cannot properly express how drastic and violent the power of God hit me.

As I lay on the ground, my sight had become slightly dim. I saw a figure of a man walking towards me from the left. He seemed to be wearing the brown robes of a Prophet. I knew in my heart he was a Prophet. I could not see his face because there was a foggy glow that was emanating from his face. A bright light was shining from behind him. He stopped in front of me. And he said to me, **Stand upon Thy Feet O Son of Man**. The minute these words left his mouth it was like as if someone grabbed me violently by my shirt collar, and jerked me to my feet. My whole body was trembling and weak.

After I was on my feet, this Prophet held out a small wooden bowl made of acacia wood. (This word came to me in my mind) I can still see the bold white and brown grains swirling around that bowl inside and out.

The Prophet commanded me to eat of its contents. I looked into the bowl, and there in the bottom were approximately a dozen almonds. They were sliced long

Dr. Michael H Yeager

ways in very thin strips. They were moist and slightly green. I reached forth my right hand, because the Rod was now in my left hand. I scraped up about half of these almonds strips and stuck them into my mouth. As I completed this task the unknown Prophet turned his back on me, and walked away.

As I chewed these almonds strips they released a very bitter taste in my mouth. And as I chewed these almonds and swallowed, all that was around me suddenly disappeared. I found myself looking into the heavens again. But now there was nothing but darkness above me. The heavens were totally empty of all-stars and lights. Nothing but empty blackness as far as my eyes could see. I noticed a motion off to my right. I saw like a small seed of light beginning to be formed. As it began to grow, I saw that it was a letter. The Letter was an **H**. as the letter **H**. continued to grow, blood was covering it, flowing into it, out of it, and through it. It was filled with the brilliant shimmering living, quickening blood of Jesus Christ. I knew that it was the blood which I had drank. This **H**. was living, active and growing.

I also noticed a motion off to my left. There in the darkness was another H. forming and growing. But this letter **H**. had a sense of evil and darkness about it. It was covered and dripping in a putrid, dead and stinking blood. As each one of these letters continued to grow, there was a separation taking place. They were growing farther and farther apart from one another. The letter **H**. to my right was filling the heavens with light, love and life. But the **H**. to my left was filled with deception, death and misery.

As I continued to watch this unfold before my eyes, suddenly the voice of God came thundering from the heavens. This is what I Heard Him Say to me:

My Holy Church!

I knew he was speaking pertaining to the H. on my right hand side. After a pause he said

The Harlot Church!

This he was speaking pertaining to the H. on my left hand side.

I began to weep uncontrollably in my dream. I knew in my heart that it was 3 AM in the morning. As I opened my eyes, (wide awake) tears were rolling down my face. It was **3:12** in the morning.

Let him that has an ear, hear what the Spirit is saying to His Holy church!

Dr. Michael H Yeager

CHAPTER 2
UNDERSTANDING THE DREAM

14 For God speaketh once, yea twice, yet man perceiveth it not.15 In a dream, in a vision of the night,when deep sleep falleth upon men, in slumberings upon the bed;16 Then he openeth the ears of men, and sealeth their instruction,17 That he may withdraw man from his purpose, and hide pride from man.18 He keepeth back his soul from the pit, and his life from perishing by the sword. Job 33:14-18 (KJV)

6 And he said, Hear now my words: If there be a prophet among you, I the LORD will make myself known unto him in a vision, and will speak unto him in a dream. Num 12:6 (KJV)

28 The prophet that hath a dream, let him tell a dream; and he that hath my word, let him speak my word faithfully. What is the chaff to the wheat? saith the LORD.29 Is not my word like as a fire? saith the LORD; and like a hammer that breaketh the rock in pieces? Jer 23:28-29 (KJV)

18 Now as he was speaking with me, I was in a deep sleep on my face toward the ground: but he touched me, and set me upright. Dan 8:18 (KJV)

1 It is not expedient for me doubtless to glory. I will come to visions and revelations of the Lord.2 I knew a man in

Christ above fourteen years ago, (whether in the body, I cannot tell; or whether out of the body, I cannot tell: God knoweth;) such an one caught up to the third heaven.3 And I knew such a man, (whether in the body, or out of the body, I cannot tell: God knoweth;)4 How that he was caught up into paradise, and heard unspeakable words, which it is not lawful for a man to utter. 2 Cor 12:1-4 (KJV)

A work of the Spirit!

28 And it shall come to pass afterward, that I will pour out my spirit upon all flesh; and your sons and your daughters shall prophesy, your old men shall dream dreams, your young men shall see visions:

29 And also upon the servants and upon the handmaids in those days will I pour out my spirit. Joel 2:28-29 (KJV)

I believe this dream was a prophetic word of what is about to happen!

1 The Revelation of Jesus Christ, which God gave unto him, to shew unto his servants things which must shortly come to pass; and he sent and signified it by his angel unto his servant John: Rev 1:1 (KJV)

19 Write the things which thou hast seen, and the things which are, and the things which shall be hereafter; Rev 1:19 (KJV)

13 Howbeit when he, the Spirit of truth, is come, he will guide you into all truth: for he shall not speak of himself; but whatsoever he shall hear, that shall he speak: and he will shew you things to come. John 16:13 (KJV)

CHAPTER 3
SHAKING OF HEAVEN & EARTH

In this Dream I found myself standing outside of a small town on top of a grass covered hill. Other saints (some that I am familiar with) were gathered together there with me. (There were seven to a dozen of us). The stars were shining brightly from above. There was no moon this particular night. It was a beautiful warm summer evening. You could hear the night life all around us. The crickets and frogs were joined together in their song. As I was standing there with the gathering of these saints, I sensed in my heart that something astounding was about to happen in the heavens above us.

15 Then a spirit passed before my face; the hair of my flesh stood up: Job 4:15 (KJV)

Many times in my life I have had such experiences, Perceiving that God is about to do something right before it happens! I would like to give to you two examples.

On August 1, 2007 my wife, three sons and daughter and I were traveling on Highway I 35 W. We were in a crew cab pickup truck, pulling a 35 foot fifth wheel trailer. We were headed into the downtown area of Minneapolis Minnesota. As I was driving, I sensed in my

Dr. Michael H Yeager

heart that we needed to get off this highway, even though our GPS was taking us the shortest route to where we were headed. I informed my family that something was wrong, there was a quickening in my heart, and we needed to get off this highway. I took the nearest exit and went north. After a while we connected to another highway, and headed west. Later in the afternoon we pulled into a store to take a break from driving. As we entered this facility we noticed that people were gathered around the TV. We could see that some major disaster had taken place. The viewer's informed us that a bridge had collapsed over the Mississippi River earlier in the day. It was I 35 W. which we had been traveling on. If we had not left the highway when we did we most likely would have been on that bridge when it collapse.

My second illustration took place about a year later, June 9, 2008. My family and I were ministering at Wisconsin Dells in Wisconsin. I was ministering to an Indian tribe that had invited us to come and speak. On the second night of these meetings God was moving in a wonderful marvelous way, but as I finished speaking the spirit of God spoke to my heart and told me that we needed to leave that night. I knew in my heart that this was God. I informed the leadership that had arranged these meetings for us that we would have to be canceling the rest of the meetings. They were upset, in which I could understand. My wife and children were also upset. My family reminded me that I was never one to cancel meetings. I informed them all the I knew this was the case, but I knew in my heart that we needed to leave. After we left the meeting my family asked if we could leave the next morning? It was raining rather heavy and

12

they did not want to get wet and drive through the night. I told them that no, we had to leave. As we were passing by the dam at Dell Lake where we had been camping we notice that the water was running rapidly alongside the dam. We drove through the whole night back to Pennsylvania. The next day one of our parishioners asked us if we had heard about what had taken place in the early morning in Wisconsin? I asked them to explain what they were talking about. They informed us that the dam at Dell Lake had collapsed. The whole Lake burst forth over the town. To this day you can watch videos of that disaster on the Internet. If I had not heard the voice of God , my family and I would most likely have been drowned.

I perceived that the heavens were about to be shaken. I perceived in my heart that it was necessary for all of us to immediately get on our backs, and look into the heavens. When I shared this with those who were gathered together with me on the Hill, they all agreed and we immediately laid down on our backs. Within just a matter of minutes the heavens above us exploded into activity. It was as if a great battle was unfolding in the heavens. There was destruction

happening throughout the sky as if it was in great travail and pain, and yet that there was a birthing, a coming forth of life and a new heaven.

30 And I will shew wonders in the heavens and in the earth, blood, and fire, and pillars of smoke.
31 The sun shall be turned into darkness, and the moon

into blood, before the great and the terrible day of the LORD come.³² And it shall come to pass, that whosoever shall call on the name of the LORD shall be delivered: for in mount Zion and in Jerusalem shall be deliverance, as the LORD hath said, and in the remnant whom the LORD shall call. Joel 2:30-32 (KJV)

11 And great earthquakes shall be in divers places, and famines, and pestilences; and fearful sights and great signs shall there be from heaven.¹² But before all these, they shall lay their hands on you, and persecute you, delivering you up to the synagogues, and into prisons, being brought before kings and rulers for my name's sake.¹³ And it shall turn to you for a testimony. Luke 21:11-13 (KJV) **10-28**

(I believe we are entering into those days)

25 And there shall be signs in the sun, and in the moon, and in the stars; and upon the earth distress of nations, with perplexity; the sea and the waves roaring;²⁶ Men's hearts failing them for fear, and for looking after those

things which are coming on the earth: for the powers of heaven shall be shaken. Luke 21:25-26 (KJV)

29 Immediately after the tribulation of those days shall the sun be darkened, and the moon shall not give her light, and the stars shall fall from heaven, and the powers of the heavens shall be shaken: Matt 24:29 (KJV)

At the time of his dream I had not realized what was happening in the heavens with our Sun ,(Lunar and solar eclipses). If I understand correctly we will see things in the heavens that the scientists say will not be repeated for another 2000 years. And that we will have massive solar flares from now up into 2015. That these solar flares according to NASA will have the potential of destroying our whole grid system, sending us back into the dark ages.

.   **What we watched unfold before us was mind boggling and dumbfounding. Frightening and yet exhilarating. It seemed to go on for hours. And as fast as it had begun, it was over with. All of us present slowly arose to our feet. We were so overwhelmed and dumbfounded with what we saw that none of us could talk. We were utterly speechless. Our hearts were filled with wonder and amazement. I perceived that all who were present knew that God was revealing himself to the human race in a way He had not previously demonstrated. That God was doing**

something in the heavens and the earth that humanity had not yet seen or experienced.

TWO MAJOR EVENTS

#1 The Gathering of God's People!

#2 The Return of Jesus Christ!

Dr. Michael H Yeager

18 And on my servants and on my handmaidens I will pour out in those days of my Spirit; and they shall prophesy:19 And I will shew wonders in heaven above, and signs in the earth beneath; blood, and fire, and vapour of smoke:20 The sun shall be turned into darkness, and the moon into blood, before that great and notable day of the Lord come:21 And it shall come to pass, that whosoever shall call on the name of the Lord shall be saved. Acts 2:18-21 (KJV)

7 Be patient therefore, brethren, unto the coming of the Lord. Behold, the husbandman waiteth for the precious fruit of the earth, and hath long patience for it, until he receive the early and latter rain.
   James 5:7 (KJV)

Major happenings in the heavens!

After this experience, this dream, I asked the Lord what it was that I was seeing? He informed me that this was the great migration. I asked him what he meant by that? He informed me that all of nature and creation is an illustration of his will, plans and purposes. And that when we watch nature as the fish return to their spawning grounds, flocks of birds fly south, and insects come bursting forth at certain seasons, I believe this is an illustration of what will happen with the ingathering of God's people. Instead of calling this book The Great Awakening, it could be called The Great Migration.

That the beginning of this great migration would be terrible signs, sights and wonders in the heavens. And in order for there to be a great gathering of the saints there must first be an out pouring of tremendous divine fear upon humanity. All true revival begins with a revelation of the awesomeness of God. This will produce overwhelming fear. There will be one of two responses from this experience. Some will come running to God as fast as they can like the prodigal son coming back to his father. Others will run to the caves and the dens of the earth trying to hide themselves from God's wrath and anger.

CHAPTER 4
THE HEAVENS ROLLED AWAY

We all dispersed from the hilltop slowly going our own separate ways. I found myself on a sidewalk beginning to enter into a small community. The streets were filled with people looking into the heavens. I could see great fear filling the faces on those who were speaking back and forth to one another in whispers about what all of this could mean? I continued to walk down the sidewalk not speaking to anyone. The atmosphere was filled with a sense of great fear and anticipation.

11 And great fear came upon all the church, and upon as many as heard these things. Acts 5:11 (KJV)

17 And this was known to all the Jews and Greeks also dwelling at Ephesus; and fear fell on them all, and the name of the Lord Jesus was magnified. 18 And many that believed came, and confessed, and shewed their deeds. Acts 19:17-18 (KJV)

I believe with all my heart that this visitation is a

Dr. Michael H Yeager

revelation of the great fear that will come upon the earth.
First I believe that the fear of the Lord will come back in
to the church, the body of Christ, the bride of Jesus. But
then there will be those instead of repenting will run from
God. When they should be running to God crying for
mercy and help. If they would run to God, he would have
mercy upon them, embracing them in his loving arms.

**As I entered deeper into this town, once again I
sense that something was about to happen. (Now this
is where it really begins to get interesting.)The minute
I perceived something dramatic was about to happen
I stopped. There were tall buildings off to my right
and left hand, which you would typically find in a
small town.**

*1 Now it came to pass in the thirtieth year, in the fourth
month, in the fifth day of the month, as I was among the
captives by the river of Chebar, that the heavens were
opened, and I saw visions of God.
  Ezek 1:1 (KJV)*

*16 And Jesus, when he was baptized, went up straightway
out of the water: and, lo, the heavens were opened unto
him, and he saw the Spirit of God descending like a dove,
and lighting upon him:
17 And lo a voice from heaven, saying, This is my
beloved Son, in whom I am well pleased.
  Matt 3:16-17 (KJV)*

51 And he saith unto him, Verily, verily, I say unto you, Hereafter ye shall see heaven open, and the angels of God ascending and descending upon the Son of man. John 1:51 (KJV)

55 But he, being full of the Holy Ghost, looked up stedfastly into heaven, and saw the glory of God, and Jesus standing on the right hand of God,56 And said, Behold, I see the heavens opened, and the Son of man standing on the right hand of God. Acts 7:55-56 (KJV)

9 On the morrow, as they went on their journey, and drew nigh unto the city, Peter went up upon the housetop to pray about the sixth hour:0 And he became very hungry, and would have eaten: but while they made ready, he fell into a trance,11 And saw heaven opened, and a certain vessel descending unto him, as it had been a great sheet knit at the four corners, and let down to the earth: Acts 10:9-11 (KJV)

1 After this I looked, and, behold, a door was opened in heaven: and the first voice which I heard was as it were of a trumpet talking with me; which said, Come up hither, and I will shew thee things which must be hereafter. Rev 4:1 (KJV)

11 And I saw heaven opened, and behold a white horse; and he that sat upon him was called Faithful and True, and in righteousness he doth judge and make war. Rev 19:11 (KJV)

I looked up into the heavens, and it seemed as if to me the heavens were made from a parchment. I watched in amazement as if an invisible hand was rolling up the heavens like they were a newspaper, or a parchment. And then as if the heavens were insignificant, it was set aside as if it were nothing.

13 And the stars of heaven fell unto the earth, even as a fig tree casteth her untimely figs, when she is shaken of a mighty wind. 14 And the heaven departed as a scroll when it is rolled together; and every mountain and island were moved out of their places. Rev 6:13-14 (KJV)

25 Of old hast thou laid the foundation of the earth: and the heavens are the work of thy hands.

26 They shall perish, but thou shalt endure. yea, all of them shall wax old like a garment; as a vesture shalt thou change them, and they shall be changed: 27 But thou art the same, and thy years shall have no end. Psalms 102:25-27 (KJV)

4 And all the host of heaven shall be dissolved, and the heavens shall be rolled together as a scroll: and all their host shall fall down, as the leaf falleth off from the vine, and as a falling fig from the fig tree. Isaiah 34:4 (KJV)

10 And, Thou, Lord, in the beginning hast laid the foundation of the earth; and the heavens are the works of thine hands:11 They shall perish; but thou remainest; and they all shall wax old as doth a garment;12 And as a vesture shalt thou fold them up, and they shall be changed: but thou art the same, and thy years shall not fail. Heb 1:10-12 (KJV)

33 Heaven and earth shall pass away: but my words shall not pass away. Luke 21:33 (KJV)

This particular part of my dream dramatically touched and changed my life. I knew that the Scriptures have declared that God would roll up the heavens like a scroll, but I never imagined it was so literal! I always thought it simply meant the first heavens. (the atmospheric heaven around the earth)

When I ask the Lord about this dramatic event, He reminded me that he had created all of the solar systems, galaxy's and universe in one day. And that he had specifically created it for times and seasons, signs and wonders in the earth. And the specific purpose for which he had created the heavens above were about to be fulfilled. That the heavens themselves will be used as the great trumpet call to bring home Gods prodigal sons and daughters.

Dr. Michael H Yeager

That God himself is so amazing and awesome that in one day he created all of the universe, galaxies, solar systems around us. And from then until now all of the universe is still expanding to such an extent that even with modern technology we are not able to even come close to investigating by telescopes even a fraction of its expansion. Oh how we have underestimated who God really is!

Genesis 1: 14 And God said , Let there be lights in the firmament of the heaven to divide the day from the night; and let them be for signs, and for seasons, and for days, and years: 15 And let them be for lights in the firmament of the heaven to give light upon the earth: and it was so. 16 And God made two great lights; the greater light to rule the day, and the lesser light to rule the night: he made the stars also. 17 And God set them in the firmament of the heaven to give light upon the earth, 18 And to rule over the day and over the night, and to divide the light from the darkness: and God saw that it was good. 19 And the evening and the morning were the fourth day.

CHAPTER 5
THE LAMB OF GOD

The minute this took place behind where the heavens had been there was now an innumerable multitude of the heavenly host. The Saints of all ages dressed in glistening white, were gathered with the angelic armies behind them. In the midst was the Heavenly Father sitting upon a great white throne. God the Father was huge in size in that all else looked small in comparison.

11 And I saw a great white throne, and him that sat on it, from whose face the earth and the heaven fled away; and there was found no place for them. Rev 20:11 (KJV)

All of those who were present including the Father seemed to be looking off to my right. As I looked in the direction in which they were gazing to my amazement there was the Lamb of God.

12 Saying with a loud voice, Worthy is the Lamb that was slain to receive power, and riches, and wisdom, and strength, and honour, and glory, and blessing.13 And every creature which is in heaven, and on the earth, and under the earth, and such as are in the sea, and all that are in them, heard I saying, Blessing, and honour, and glory, and power, be unto him that sitteth upon the throne, and unto the Lamb for ever and ever. Rev 5:12-13 (KJV)

From this moment forward the emphasis is Jesus Christ

His wool was glistening white as snow. He was lying upon His side as if He had been slain. His backside was away from me, His underside toward me. And out from His rib, (the third rib) from his side flowed a stream of bright shimmering living, quickening blood. Directly in front of His body there had formed a pool of this living blood. I knew there was no bottom to this pool of blood. It is hard to explain what I sensed in my heart as I looked upon His, the Lamb of God's precious living blood.

6 And I beheld, and, lo, in the midst of the throne and of the four beasts, and in the midst of the elders, stood a Lamb as it had been slain, having seven horns and seven eyes, which are the seven Spirits of God sent forth into all the earth. Rev 5:6 (KJV)

8 And all that dwell upon the earth shall worship him, whose names are not written in the book of life of the Lamb slain from the foundation of the world. Rev 13:8 (KJV)

12 Wherefore Jesus also, that he might sanctify the people with his own blood, suffered without the gate. Heb13:12 (KJV)

18 Forasmuch as ye know that ye were not redeemed with corruptible things, as silver and gold, from your vain conversation received by tradition from your fathers;19 But with the precious blood of Christ, as of a lamb without blemish and without spot: 1 Peter 1:18-19 (KJV)

By his blood, in his blood, through his blood, because of his blood:

#1 Access to the Heavenly Father

#2 Authority

#3Boldness

#4 Cleansed

#5 Confidence

#6 Delivered

#7 Forgiveness

#8 Freedom

#9 Inheritance

#10 Justified

#11 Life

#12 Mercy

Dr. Michael H Yeager

#13 New Covenant

#14 New Creatures

#15 Pardon

#16 Power

#17 Protection

#18 Provision

#19 Ransomed

#20 Redeemed

#21 Sanctified

A. Redemption.

1. Acts 20:28 - "church of God purchased with His own blood"

    2. Eph. 1:7 - "we have redemption through His blood"

    3. I Pet. 1:9 - "redeemed...with precious blood"

    4. Rev. 5:9 - "purchased for God with His blood, men from every tribe"

B. Propitiation.

    1. Rom. 3:25 - "God displayed Jesus as a propitiation in His blood"

C. Cleansing.

    1. Heb. 9:14 - "blood of Christ...will cleanse your conscience"

    2. I John 1:7 - "blood of Jesus cleanses us from all sin"

    3. Rev. 7:14 - "washed their robes in the blood of the Lamb"

D. Forgiveness.

    1. Eph. 1:7 - "redemption through His blood, the forgiveness of our trespasses"

    2. Heb. 9:22 - "without shedding of blood there is no forgiveness"

    3. Rev. 1:5 - "released us from our sins by His blood"

E. Access to God.

    1. Eph. 2:13 - "brought near to God by the blood of Christ"

    2. Heb. 10:19 - "confidence to enter Holy Place by blood of Jesus"

F. Reconciliation.

    1. Col. 1:20 - "reconciled, made pace through the blood of the cross"

G. Justification.
1. Rom. 5:9 - "having been justified by his blood"
H. Sanctification.
1. Heb. 13:12 - "that He might sanctify the people through His blood"
I. Conquest of evil.
1. Rev. 12:11 - "overcame...because of the blood of the Lamb"
J. Basis of new covenant.
1. Heb. 13:20 - "through the blood of the eternal covenant"
K. Lord's Supper
1. Matt. 26:28 - "This is the new covenant in My blood"
2. I Cor. 10:16 - "the cup of blessing...a sharing in the blood of Christ"

CHAPTER 6
THE ROD OF JESSE

As I was looking upon this pool of precious blood, I felt something manifest itself in my right hand. I looked down, and there in my right hand was a branch, a ROD. (This was the specific word that came to my mind)This was not just any ordinary Rod. It was absolutely straight, and it was made of Olive Wood, seemingly seven feet tall. (These are things I just knew to be true)

1 And there shall come forth a rod out of the stem of Jesse, and a Branch shall grow out of his roots:
2 And the spirit of the LORD shall rest upon him, the spirit of wisdom and understanding, the spirit of counsel and might, the spirit of knowledge and of the fear of the LORD; Isaiah 11:1-2 (KJV)

5 Behold, the days come, saith the LORD, that I will raise unto David a righteous Branch, and a King shall reign and prosper, and shall execute judgment and justice in the earth. Jer 23:5 (KJV)

15 In those days, and at that time, will I cause the Branch of righteousness to grow up unto David; and he shall execute judgment and righteousness in the land. Jer 33:15 (KJV)

8 Hear now, O Joshua the high priest, thou, and thy fellows that sit before thee: for they are men wondered at: for, behold, I will bring forth my servant the BRANCH. Zech 3:8 (KJV)

This rod is a type of: Jesus Christ, the name of Christ, divine authority, miraculous power, God's anger and retribution, God's guidance and gentleness, God's eternal word, his healing power represented by the brazen serpent on the rod, and the cross of Calvary.

This Rob was absolutely straight revealing the divine character and nature of Jesus Christ. That he was tempted in every way as we are and yet without sin There is no crookedness or sinfulness in Jesus Christ.

This Rob was made of olive wood from an olive tree. It is called the 'tree of oil." It is from a primitive root meaning "to shine." It is a remarkable plant in regards to its oil, its wood, its ancient usage, ordinary in appearance and size – some might even say a little bit "ugly,"

"It is an evergreen, if the trunk is cut down, the shoots from its roots continue to grow ,Olive wood is very hard, and beautifully grained,

The olive branch has been a symbol of "peace "for instance the dove returned to Noah's ark carrying an olive branch .

The holy anointing oil ,"oil for the light" (Exo.25:6). "When you beat your olive trees, Pure beaten olive oil was the best in quality. The oil represents the holy anointing by the power of the Spirit of God.

It is also , regarded as "the king of trees."

<u>This is all symbolic of Jesus Christ</u>

Immediately I knew what I was to do with this Rod in my right hand.

2 And the LORD said unto him, What is that in thine hand? And he said, A rod. Ex 4:2 (KJV)

17 And thou shalt take this rod in thine hand, wherewith thou shalt do signs. Ex 4:17 (KJV)

4 But with righteousness shall he judge the poor, and reprove with equity for the meek of the earth: and he shall smite the earth with the rod of his mouth, and with the breath of his lips shall he slay the wicked. Isaiah 11:4 (KJV)

2 The LORD shall send the rod of thy strength out of Zion: rule thou in the midst of thine enemies. Psalms 110:2 (KJV)

staff, branch, tribe (of vine)

9 And Moses said unto Joshua, Choose us out men, and go out, fight with Amalek: tomorrow I will stand on the top of the hill with the rod of God in mine hand. Ex 17:9 (KJV)

21 times in EXODUS Moses used the rod!

With the rod in the hand of Moses were performed all of the signs and wonders. The rod became a Snake, water to blood, frogs, lice, hail & fire, locust, when he struck the rock with the rod it split were the right and water came gushing out. He also defeated the enemies of God with the rod by which the Lord gave them Victory over the enemies.

I lifted this Rod towards the pool of blood in the heavens. To my amazement it seemed to be just the right length to reach into the blood. This blood was in the heavens, and yet this seven foot Rod was able to reach the precious blood of Jesus.

The number seven has tremendous significance for instance John the revelator seen the evidence of this many times in his heavenly visitation.

The book of Revelations beautifully reveals the Number Seven in this regards:

> Seven churches
> Seven Spirits of God
> Seven golden candlesticks
> Seven stars
> Seven lamps
> Seven seals
> Seven eyes
> Seven horns
> Seven angels

Seven trumpets
Seven heads
Seven crowns
Seven plagues
Seven gold vials
Seven mountains
Seven kings
Seven thunder's

God's Spiritual perfection comes in His revelation of the number seven.

CHAPTER 7
THE SPIRIT & THE BLOOD

I put the end of the Rod right into this pool of living blood. The blood immediately flowed to the end of the Rod. This living blood wrapped itself around the end of the Rod as if it was in absolute oneness with the Rod. Then with my right hand I pulled the Rod back towards me. Once the Rod was back into my Realm (I do not know how else to explain it). I directed the end of the Rod towards my mouth. It looked as if the blood was going to fall off from the end of the Rod. But not a drop fell to the ground.

The blood of Jesus is not merely blood, but it is "the blood of the covenant" (Hebrews 10:29; 13:20).

Redemption by the blood of Jesus is in Christ (Eph. 1:7). To be in Christ is the same as being in his body which is the church (Col. 1:2; 3:15; 1:18). Therefore, salvation by the blood of Jesus is in his church.

Exodus 12:23, "And the blood shall be to you for a token upon the houses where ye are: and when I see the blood, I will pass over you, and the plague shall not be upon you to destroy you, when I smite the land of Egypt." Did you read that ... WHEN I SEE THE BLOOD!!!

Dr. Michael H Yeager

Hebrews 9:24-26 state, "For Christ is not entered into the holy places made with hands, which are the figures of the true; but into heaven itself, now to appear in the presence of God for us..." (that is, God the Father). Jesus took His shed blood to Heaven to present unto the Father, by applying it to the Mercy Seat

Hebrews 9:12, "Neither by the blood of goats and calves, but by his own blood he entered in once into the holy place, having obtained eternal redemption for us

The significance of the blood of Christ is so profound that we could easily write a book on just this particular subject alone. Without the shedding of the blood of Jesus Christ (God in the flesh) there could be no salvation. If even the blood of Abel still cries out from the ground, then what is the blood of Christ doing for us. I declare to you that the blood of Christ is still living, active, and redeeming those who take it by faith.

CHAPTER 8
DRINKING HIS BLOOD,

I opened my mouth wide, and stuck the end of the Rod with the Living Blood into my mouth. I drank all of the blood which had been on the Rod. The very moment that I drank the blood, it was as if Power exploded inside of me, knocking me flat on my back like a dead man. It slammed me violently to the ground. I cannot properly express how drastic and violent the power of God hit me.

The blood of Christ when it comes in contact with the old man, will kill him. For it is the Life of Christ himself. I truly believe that the blood of Christ is the Holy Ghost. It is the spirit of the living God personified in God's people.

11 For the life of the flesh is in the blood: and I have given it to you upon the altar to make an atonement for your souls: for it is the blood that maketh an atonement for the soul. Lev 17:11 (KJV)

14 For it is the life of all flesh; the blood of it is for the life thereof: therefore I said unto the children of Israel, Ye shall eat the blood of no manner of flesh: for the life of all flesh is the blood thereof: whosoever eateth it shall be cut off. Lev 17:14 (KJV)

23 Only be sure that thou eat not the blood: for the blood is the life; and thou mayest not eat the life with the flesh. Deut 12:23 (KJV)

20 But that we write unto them, that they abstain from pollutions of idols, and from fornication, and from things strangled, and from blood. Acts 15:20 (KJV)

29 That ye abstain from meats offered to idols, and from blood, and from things strangled, and from fornication: from which if ye keep yourselves, ye shall do well. Fare ye well. Acts 15:29 (KJV)

25 As touching the Gentiles which believe, we have written and concluded that they observe no such thing, save only that they keep themselves from things offered to idols, and from blood, and from strangled, and from fornication. Acts 21:25 (KJV)

3 For ye are dead, and your life is hid with Christ in God. Col 3:3 (KJV)

16 This I say then, Walk in the Spirit, and ye shall not fulfil the lust of the flesh. Gal 5:16 (KJV)

53 Then Jesus said unto them, Verily, verily, I say unto you, Except ye eat the flesh of the Son of man, and drink his blood, ye have no life in you.54 Whoso eateth my flesh, and drinketh my blood, hath eternal life; and I will raise him up at the last day. John 6:53-54 (KJV)

27 And he took the cup, and gave thanks, and gave it to them, saying, Drink ye all of it; Matt 26:27 (KJV)

11 And they overcame him by the blood of the Lamb, and by the word of their testimony; and they loved not their lives unto the death. Rev 12:11 (KJV)

14 And I said unto him, Sir, thou knowest. And he said to me, These are they which came out of great tribulation, and have washed their robes, and made them white in the blood of the Lamb. Rev 7:14 (KJV)

As I lay on the ground, my sight had become slightly dim. I saw a figure of a man walking towards me from the left. He seemed to be wearing the brown

robes of a Prophet. I knew in my heart he was a Prophet. I could not see his face because there was a

foggy glow that was emanating from his face. A bright light was shining from behind him. He stopped in front of me. And he said to me, Stand upon Thy Feet O Son of Man. The minute these words left his mouth it was like as if someone grabbed me violently by my shirt collar, and jerked me to my feet. My whole body was trembling and weak.

1 And he said unto me, Son of man, stand upon thy feet, and I will speak unto thee.

2 And the spirit entered into me when he spake unto me, and set me upon my feet, that I heard him that spake unto me. Ezek 2:1-2 (KJV)

11 And he said unto me, O Daniel, a man greatly beloved, understand the words that I speak unto thee, and stand upright: for unto thee am I now sent. And when he had spoken this word unto me, I stood trembling. Dan 10:11 (KJV)

16 But rise, and stand upon thy feet: for I have appeared unto thee for this purpose, to make thee a minister and a witness both of these things which thou hast seen, and of those things in the which I will appear unto thee; Acts 26:16 (KJV)

CHAPTER 9
ARK OF THE COVENANT

After I was on my feet, this Prophet held out a small wooden bowl made of acacia wood. (This word came to me in my mind)

In the King James version this what is commonly called shittim. It is this particular tree that God had Moses built and crafted all of the furnishings in the holy of holies! Including the ark of the covenant. We shall see that the ark is a type of Jesus Christ, God manifested in the flesh . In the Old Testament typology -this particular tree is a thorny trees –(Exodus 25:10 -ark of shittim wood) - if you did a little bit of research there is a belief that Christ's "crown of thorns" was made from acacia, the shittim tree. This particular tree is extremely durable, hard, tough, has good strength and flexible qualities, is immunized against dry rots and insect pest, Unprotected and untreated will last 40 years.

I can still see the bold white and brown grains swirling around that bowl.

5 But he was wounded for our transgressions, he was bruised for our iniquities: the chastisement of our peace was upon him; and with his stripes we are healed. Isaiah

53:5 (KJV)

24 Who his own self bare our sins in his own body on the tree, that we, being dead to sins, should live unto righteousness: by whose stripes ye were healed. 1 Peter 2:24 (KJV)

The Prophet commanded me to eat of its contents.

26 And as they were eating, Jesus took bread, and blessed it, and brake it, and gave it to the disciples, and said, Take, eat; this is my body. Matt 26:26 (KJV)

1 Moreover he said unto me, Son of man, eat that thou findest; eat this roll, and go speak unto the house of Israel.2 So I opened my mouth, and he caused me to eat that roll.3 And he said unto me, Son of man, cause thy belly to eat, and fill thy bowels with this roll that I give thee. Then did I eat it; and it was in my mouth as honey for sweetness. Ezek 3:1-3 (KJV)

I looked into the bowl, and there in the bottom was approximately a dozen almonds. They were sliced long ways in thin strips. They were moist and slightly green.

Almonds are a symbol of Christ's resurrection," it means a hastening," is given to it on the account of almond trees putting forth their blossoms so early, generally in February. Plus Aaron's rod yielded almonds(Num. 17:8; Heb. 9:4). God also instructed Moses to make certain parts of the candlestick for the ark of carved work were "like unto almonds" (Ex. 25:33, 34) It is commonly the first fruit tree to blossom in the new year!

Of course the number 12 is extremely significant also in that it could represent the 12 tribes, the 12 apostles, the 12 gates of the new Jerusalem, the 12 foundations of Jerusalem.

I reached forth my right hand, because the Rod was now in my left hand. I scraped up about half of these almonds strips and stuck them into my mouth. As I completed this task the unknown Prophet turned his back on me, and walked away.

As I chewed these almonds strips they released a very bitter taste in my mouth.

After this experience I discovered that there are two different types of almond trees. One is a domesticated tree which produces sweet almonds. Now sweet almonds represent a prosperous, joyful easy journey. The other

Dr. Michael H Yeager

type of almond tree is considered a wild almond tree. The almonds of this particular tree are bitter and represent tribulation, trials, difficulties. Paul declared that we must through much tribulation enter into the kingdom of heaven.

9 And I went unto the angel, and said unto him, Give me the little book. And he said unto me, Take it, and eat it up; and it shall make thy belly bitter, but it shall be in thy mouth sweet as honey.

10 And I took the little book out of the angel's hand, and ate it up; and it was in my mouth sweet as honey: and as soon as I had eaten it, my belly was bitter. 11 And he said unto me, Thou must prophesy again before many peoples, and nations, and tongues, and kings. Rev 10:9-11 (KJV)

And as I chewed these almonds and swallowed, all that was around me suddenly disappeared. I found myself looking into the heavens again. But now there was nothing but darkness above me. The heavens were totally empty of all-stars and lights. Nothing but empty blackness as far as my eyes could see.

10 For the stars of heaven and the constellations thereof shall not give their light: the sun shall be darkened in his going forth, and the moon shall not cause her light to shine. Isaiah 13:10 (KJV)

15 That day is a day of wrath, a day of trouble and distress, a day of wasteness and desolation, a day of darkness and gloominess, a day of clouds and thick darkness, 16 A day of the trumpet and alarm against the fenced cities, and against the high towers. 17 And I will bring distress upon men, that they shall walk like blind men, because they have sinned against the LORD: and their blood shall be poured out as dust, and their flesh as the dung. Zeph 1:15-17 (KJV)

29 Immediately after the tribulation of those days shall the sun be darkened, and the moon shall not give her light, and the stars shall fall from heaven, and the powers of the heavens shall be shaken:

30 And then shall appear the sign of the Son of man in heaven: and then shall all the tribes of the earth mourn, and they shall see the Son of man coming in the clouds of heaven with power and great glory.

Matt 24:29-30 (KJV)

Dr. Michael H Yeager

CHAPTER 10
Holy Church & Harlot Church

I noticed a motion off to my right. I saw like a small seed of light beginning to be formed.

16 I Jesus have sent mine angel to testify unto you these things in the churches. I am the root and the offspring of David, and the bright and morning star. Rev 22:16 (KJV)

Is not Jesus the seed of light planted into the soil of our souls. Does not everything come from Him, through Him, and by Him. He is our all in all, are everything!

As it began to grow, I saw that it was a letter. The Letter was an H. as the letter H. continued to grow, blood was covering it, flowing into it, out of it, and through it, around it. It was filled with the brilliant shimmering living, quickening blood of Jesus Christ. I knew that it was the blood which I had drank. This H. was living, active and growing.

I also noticed a motion off to my left. There in the darkness was another H. forming and growing.

Dr. Michael H Yeager

But this letter H. had a sense of evil and darkness about it. It was covered and dripping in a putrid, dead and stinking blood. As each one of these letters continued to grow, there was a separation taking place. They were growing farther and farther apart from one another. The letter H. to my right was filling the heavens with light, love and life. But the H. to my left was filled with deception, death and misery.

* By their fruits!!! It is so vitally important to check on our fruit. Galatians chapter five tells us what the fruits of the spirit are, which are love, joy, peace, long-suffering, gentleness, goodness, meekness, temperance, faithfulness and against such there is no law. The word of God clearly declares you can never have too much of these fruits. But then it gives us a list of the works of the flesh that manifested. And that boldly declares that they that do such things shall not inherit eternal life. Only those who have crucified the lust of the flesh will partake of eternity with God.

As I continued to watch this unfold before my eyes, suddenly the voice of God came thundering from the heavens. This is what I Heard Him Say to me: My Holy Church! I knew he was speaking pertaining to the H. on my right hand side. There is unfathomable joy and love in his voice!

The Coming Great Awakening

27 That he might present it to himself a glorious church, not having spot, or wrinkle, or any such thing; but that it should be holy and without blemish. Eph 5:27 (KJV)

13 The king's daughter is all glorious within: her clothing is of wrought gold. Psalms 45:13 (KJV)

3 Thou shalt also be a crown of glory in the hand of the LORD, and a royal diadem in the hand of thy God. Isaiah 62:3 (KJV)

10 And he carried me away in the spirit to a great and high mountain, and shewed me that great city, the holy Jerusalem, descending out of heaven from God, Rev 21:10 (KJV)

10 Hearken, O daughter, and consider, and incline thine ear; forget also thine own people, and thy father's house; 11 So shall the king greatly desire thy beauty: for he is thy Lord; and worship thou him. Psalms 45:10-11 (KJV)

9 But ye are a chosen generation, a royal priesthood, an holy nation, a peculiar people; that ye should shew forth the praises of him who hath called you out of darkness into his marvellous light: 10 Which in time past were not a people, but are now the people of God: which had not obtained mercy, but now have obtained mercy. 1 Peter 2:9-10 (KJV)

Proverbs 31 gives us a perfect description of the brighter the body of Christ. Read the following verses with the perspective that this is God's glorious church.

10 Who can find a virtuous woman? for her price is far above rubies.

11 The heart of her husband doth safely trust in her, so that he shall have no need of spoil.

12 She will do him good and not evil all the days of her life.

13 She seeketh wool, and flax, and worketh willingly with her hands.

14 She is like the merchants' ships; she bringeth her food from afar.

15 She riseth also while it is yet night, and giveth meat to her household, and a portion to her maidens.

16 She considereth a field, and buyeth it: with the fruit of her hands she planteth a vineyard.

17 She girdeth her loins with strength, and strengtheneth her arms.

18 She perceiveth that her merchandise is good: her candle goeth not out by night.

19 She layeth her hands to the spindle, and her hands hold the distaff.

20 She stretcheth out her hand to the poor; yea, she reacheth forth her hands to the needy.

21 She is not afraid of the snow for her household: for all her household are clothed with scarlet.

22 She maketh herself coverings of tapestry; her clothing is silk and purple.

23 Her husband is known in the gates, when he sitteth among the elders of the land.

24 She maketh fine linen, and selleth it; and delivereth girdles unto the merchant.

25 Strength and honour are her clothing; and she shall rejoice in time to come.

26 She openeth her mouth with wisdom; and in her tongue is the law of kindness.

27 She looketh well to the ways of her household, and

eateth not the bread of idleness.

28 Her children arise up, and call her blessed; her husband also, and he praiseth her.

29 Many daughters have done virtuously, but thou excellest them all.

30 Favour is deceitful, and beauty is vain: but a woman that feareth the LORD, she shall be praised.

31 Give her of the fruit of her hands; and let her own works praise her in the gates.

Prov 31:10-31 (KJV)

After a pause God's thundering voice said .... The Harlot Church! This he was speaking pertaining to the H. on my left hand side. His voice was filled with anger and disgust!

I am convinced that Proverbs 29 is a declaration of the harlot church that has sold her soul for financial gain. Mammon has become her Lord and that she is led and guided by monetary gain.

5 That they may keep thee from the strange woman, from the stranger which flattereth with her words. 6 For at the window of my house I looked through my casement,[7] And beheld among the simple ones, I discerned among the youths, a young man void of understanding,[8] Passing through the street near her corner; and he went the way to her house,[9] In the twilight, in the evening, in the black and dark night:[10] And, behold, there met him a woman with the attire of an harlot, and subtil of heart.

[11] (She is loud and stubborn; her feet abide not in her house:[12] Now is she without, now in the streets, and lieth in wait at every corner.)[13] So she caught him, and kissed him, and with an impudent face said unto him,[14] I have peace offerings with me; this day have I payed my vows.[15] Therefore came I forth to meet thee, diligently to seek thy face, and I have found thee.[16] I have decked my bed with coverings of tapestry, with carved works, with fine linen of Egypt.[17] I have perfumed my bed with myrrh, aloes, and cinnamon.[18] Come, let us take our fill of love until the morning: let us solace ourselves with loves.[19] For the goodman is not at home, he is gone a long journey: (**is this not Jesus Christ** *)[20] He hath taken a bag of money with him, and will come home at the day appointed.[21] With her much fair speech she caused him to yield, with the flattering of her lips she*

Dr. Michael H Yeager

forced him.22 He goeth after her straightway, as an ox goeth to the slaughter, or as a fool to the correction of the stocks;23 Till a dart strike through his liver; as a bird hasteth to the snare, and knoweth not that it is for his life.24 Hearken unto me now therefore, O ye children, and attend to the words of my mouth.25 Let not thine heart decline to her ways, go not astray in her paths.26 For she hath cast down many wounded: yea, many strong men have been slain by her.27 Her house is the way to hell, going down to the chambers of death.   Prov 7:5-27 (KJV)

14 The mouth of strange women is a deep pit: he that is abhorred of the LORD shall fall therein.

Prov 22:14 (KJV)

27 For a whore is a deep ditch; and a strange woman is a narrow pit. Prov 23:27 (KJV)

3 Whoso loveth wisdom rejoiceth his father: but he that keepeth company with harlots spendeth his substance. Prov 29:3 (KJV)

1 And there came one of the seven angels which had the seven vials, and talked with me, saying unto me, Come hither; I will shew unto thee the judgment of the great whore that sitteth upon many waters:2 With whom the kings of the earth have committed fornication, and the inhabitants of the earth have been made drunk with the wine of her fornication. Rev 17:1-2 (KJV)

2 For true and righteous are his judgments: for he hath judged the great whore, which did corrupt the earth with her fornication, and hath avenged the blood of his servants at her hand. Rev 19:2 (KJV)

4 Because of the multitude of the whoredoms of the wellfavoured harlot, *the mistress of witchcrafts, that selleth nations through her whoredoms, and families through her witchcrafts.5 Behold, I am against thee, saith the LORD of hosts; and I will discover thy skirts upon thy face, and I will shew the nations thy nakedness, and the kingdoms thy shame.6 And I will cast abominable filth upon thee, and make thee vile, and will set thee as a gazingstock. Nahum 3:4-6 (KJV)*

19 Now the works of the flesh are manifest, which are these; Adultery, fornication, uncleanness, lasciviousness,20 Idolatry, witchcraft, hatred, variance, emulations, wrath, strife, seditions, heresies,21 Envyings, murders, drunkenness,

Dr. Michael H Yeager

*revellings, and such like: of the which I tell you
before, as I have also told you in time past, that they
which do such things shall not inherit the kingdom of
God. Gal 5:19-21 (KJV)*

Does not Harlot a sell herself for money. Her devotion
and commitment is completely dependent upon
Monetary remunerations.

**I began to weep uncontrollably in my dream. I
knew in my heart that it was <u>3 AM</u> in the morning.
As I opened my eyes, (wide awake) tears were
rolling down my face. It was <u>3:12</u> in the morning.**

CHAPTER 11
FIELD OF DIAMONDS

The first 10 chapters of this book was the dream that I had in the spring of 2012. On the way home from a ministers conference which I was attending in Indiana on August 11 I had an open vision. At this particular conference the spirit of God confirmed to my heart that it was time for the visions and dreams he had imparted to come to pass. As I was driving home all of a sudden in front of me was a never ending field of brown dirt as far as my eyes could see. And scattered over this dirt field were different sizes of diamonds everywhere. I heard the voice of the Lord say to me : **Pick Them up!**

I said to him as I was leaning over in this vision to pick them up, Lord what are they? He responded by telling me that they were his ministry gifts. That he had scattered them throughout the land. That they had become diamonds through the hard trials, test and tribulations they had endured. He told me that if I would call them, that they would come. That their hearts had been prepared and they would be willing to minister together for the Father's glory! At the moment I felt in my heart that he wanted us to conduct a service every day. And that we would have a different minister every night ministering.

Dr. Michael H Yeager

I was up early Sunday morning walking the sanctuary of our church facility. Just crying out to God to discover his will, when he spoke to my heart again. What the Lord wanted me to do was even to a greater extent than what I had first understood. I believe at times that God cannot reveal his complete and perfect plan because it would overwhelm us. By the time the spirit oh Lord had finished speaking to me these meetings had increased from One-A-Day to at least three a day. I believe that once the spirit of revival begins to be poured out in a much more magnificent way that we will have to conduct five services a day.

Since September 1, 2012 we have been having three services every day with a different minister in each service. On the Monday after this experience I began to call spirit filled, Holy Ghost ministers to come in minister with no promise of financial remunerations. I was pleasantly surprised and blessed with the excitement that these precious brothers and sisters showed in their willingness to come and minister the truth. The spirit of the Lord also instructed me to take a specific subject for each month. September was about Jesus Christ ! October was about the Heavenly Father! November is about the Holy Spirit! December about the bride and body of Christ! January about evangelism and discipleship!

CHAPTER 12
EZEKIEL'S VISION

Ezek 37:1 The hand of the LORD was upon me, and carried me out in the spirit of the LORD, and set medown in the midst of the valley which was full of bones, **2** And caused me to pass by them roundabout: and, behold, there were very many in the open valley; and, lo, they were very dry. **3** And he said unto me, Son of man, can these bones live ? And I answered , O Lord GOD, thou knowest. **4** Again he said unto me, Prophesy upon these bones, and say unto them, O ye dry bones, hearthe word of the LORD. **5** Thus saith the Lord GOD unto these bones; Behold, I will cause breathto enter into you, and ye shall live : **6** And I will lay sinews upon you, and will bring up flesh upon you, and cover you with skin, and put breath in you, and ye shall live ; and ye shall know that I am the LORD. **7** So I prophesied as I was commanded : and as I prophesied , there was a noise, and behold a shaking, and the bones came together , bone to his bone. **8** And when I beheld , lo, thesinews and the flesh came up upon them, and the skin covered them above: but there was no

breath in them. **9** Then said he unto me, Prophesy unto
the wind, prophesy , son of man, and say to
the wind, Thus saith the Lord GOD; Come from
the four winds, O breath, and breathe upon
these slain , that they may live . **10** So I prophesied as
he commanded me, and the breath cameinto them, and
they lived , and stood up upon their feet, an
exceeding great army. **11** Then hesaid unto me, Son of
 man, these bones are the whole house of Israel:
 behold, they say , Ourbones are dried , and
our hope is lost : we are cut off for our parts.

For over two years the spirit of the Lord had
been taking me to Ezekiel 37 dealing with the Valley
of dead dry bones. Since 1983 I have been living in
the Gettysburg Pennsylvania area. It is not an area that
I would choose to live in. To be absolutely honest and
blunt with you I do not like this area one iota. And yet
the spirit of God would not allow me to leave.
According to historians over 51,000 soldiers died in
this valley, of Gettysburg. This place is surely the
Valley of dead dry bones of a historical battle that
became the turning point of the Civil War. How
amazing it is to think that God will once again cause a
mighty battle to take place were in Army is not
destroyed, but resurrected back to life. At this moment
we have over 100 ministers, many of them are pastors
of Holy Ghost spirit filled full gospel ministries from

all different backgrounds working together. Surely God is raising up his army once again to bring about a mighty revival that will not cease until the return of Christ.

ABOUT THE AUTHOR

Dr. Michael H. Yeager has been ministering God's word since 1975. The call of God upon his life has taken him too many challenging places.

You can reach him through the following:

Address:
Jesus is Lord Ministries International
3425 Chambersburg Rd.
Biglerville, Pennsylvania 17307

1-800-555-4575

Websites:

www.jilmi.org

www.docyeager.org

Dr. Michael H Yeager

www.wordbroadcast.org

www.hellsreal.com

Horrors of Hell, Splendors of Heaven
by Dr. Michael Yeager
$15.00
ISBN: 978-0-9825775-9-2

When you read the true story of Dr. Michael Yeager's encounter with the afterlife, you too will realize the indescribable depth of the horrors of hell, and the unimaginable splendors of heaven. Fall into the gut-wrenching realms of the damned, enter into the divine gates of heaven, and be escorted by an angel into an amazing dimension of beauty and nature. End your journey upon the sea of glass before the thunder and lightning of God's throne. Along the way, you will discover answers to your deepest questions about the afterlife. As you take the journey from hell to heaven and back, the revelations you receive will be eternal.

15878225R00040

Made in the USA
Charleston, SC
25 November 2012